Bedouin — The Nomads of the Desert

The Bedouin have lived as members of tribes in the deserts of the Middle East and the countries of North Africa since remote times. They have led a simple existence as nomads, living in low black tents that have provided protection against wind and sun, traveling with their camels, goats or sheep and sometimes growing a few crops. Their lifestyle has been governed by the scanty rainfall and sparse vegetation of the desert and has changed little since the days of the Old Testament characters who lived in much the same way. This book describes the Bedouin traditional way of life and shows how their lifestyles have changed rapidly in many areas due to permanent settlement in towns and alternative employment opportunities offered by the oil industry. The author, Muhammad Alotaibi, is an anthropologist who has spent many years living and working among the Bedouin people of North Africa and the Middle East.

BEDOUIN
THE NOMADS OF THE DESERT

Muhammad Alotaibi

Rourke Publications, Inc.
Vero Beach, FL 32964

Original Peoples

Eskimos — The Inuit of the Arctic
Maoris of New Zealand
Aborigines of Australia
Plains Indians of North America
South Pacific Islanders
Indians of the Andes
Indians of the Amazon
Bushmen of Central Africa
Bedouin — The Nomads of the Desert
The Zulus of Southern Africa
Lapps — Reindeer Herders of Lapland

Library of Congress Cataloging-in-Publication Data

Alotaibi, Muhammad.
  Bedouin: the nomads of the desert / Muhammad Alotaibi.
    p.   cm.—(Original peoples)
  Reprint. Originally published: Hove, East Sussex, England : Wayland, 1985.
  Bibliography: p.
  Includes index
  ISBN 0–86625–265–7
  1. Bedouins—Juvenile literature. 2. Arab countries—Social life and customs—Juvenile literature.
  I. Title.   II. Series.
[DS36.9.B4A56 1989]
956′.004927–dc19
                                88–15074
                                      CIP
                                      AC

Manufactured in Italy.
Text © 1989 Rourke Publications, Inc.

Contents

Introduction

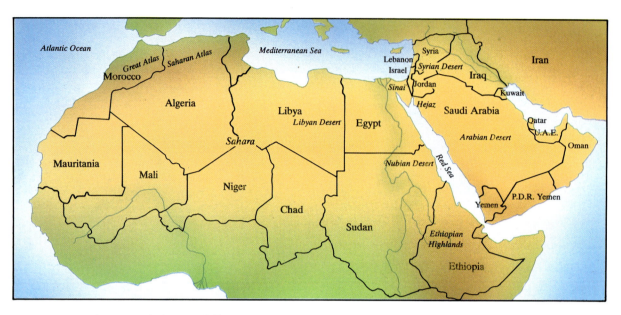

Northern Africa and the Middle East showing the deserts and countries where the Bedouin live.

The desert is a huge, silent wilderness. It is hot during the day, cold at night and invariably extremely dry. During sandstorms the sand lashes savagely at unprotected parts of the body. The stark vegetation includes drought-resistant plants such as the cactus with its prickly leaves. Roots, perhaps longer than the stem or trunk of the plant itself, search deep in the ground for moisture. Desert animals such as snakes, lizards, scorpions, toads, jerboas and elf owls manage to survive on meager diets.

It seems incredible that groups of people, such as the Bedouin, have developed lifestyles that are suited to this harsh environment. For centuries they have lived a simple, nomadic life, wandering from place to place, searching for water or grazing land for their herds, using camels as beasts of burden.

The Bedouin live in many countries in the north of Africa and the Middle East. In Africa, Bedouin are found in the Sahara Desert and in countries such as Algeria, Libya and Egypt. In the Middle East they live in Syria, Jordan, Iraq and the countries of the Arabian peninsula — especially Saudi Arabia but also Yemen, South Yemen and Oman.

This book tells the story of the Bedouin, their lifestyles in the past, far-reaching changes in their pattern of life today, and their hopes and their fears for the survival of their culture in the future. Their foremost

concerns revolve around the new occupations and living conditions that have been brought about by the exploitation of oil.

A Bedouin camp pitched in the Sinai desert. The Bedouin are skilled at surviving in this inhospitable environment.

Chapter 1 **Tribal life**

Bedouin tribes

It is estimated that there are between four million and six million Bedouin, but it is difficult to define the word Bedouin precisely. The word "Bedouin" is often used to describe all nomadic Arabs, and is derived from the Arabic word *badawiyin*, meaning "people of the desert." The Bedouin themselves believe that the word should only be used to describe camel-herding tribes rather than tribes that herd sheep and goats (known as *arab*), or settled peoples (known as *hadari*).

This Bedouin man is leading pack camels, which are used for carrying goods. Camels are very useful to the Bedouin in the desert.

Handmade goat-hair Bedouin tents in southeast Jordan.

It is thought that the Bedouin originally came from the Arabian peninsula, and later some of them moved to other deserts and to more fertile areas. Some tribes moved to the lands west of Arabia and arrived in the Sahara. They still share this territory with the nomadic Tuareg who were in that desert long before the Bedouin.

The camel herders have always regarded themselves as superior to town-dwellers, feeling that they lead a better, purer life. Some of them resist attempts made by governments to settle them in one place.

9

Bedouin men talk together with their sheikh.

Sheikhs and their tribes

The Bedouin are divided into tribes. Members of a particular tribe are known as *bani*, meaning "children of the tribe." A tribe is a complex organization that is divided into clans, each with its own chief or local sheikh. A tribe may have one clan living in Jordan, another in Iraq, and others living in different areas of Saudi Arabia. These groups may have become very different in outlook and background over the years.

The paramount sheikh is the head of the whole tribe. He comes from the most important family in the tribe and is also chief of one of the clans. The office of sheikh does not pass automatically from father to oldest son. The tribe chooses the best man available from that family.

When a new sheikh needs to be appointed and there are several possible successors, there may well be arguments and serious conflict, which might even cause whole sections of the tribe to break away.

The sheikh is regarded as a diplomat in handling the problems of others. He needs to be a man who can show courage and generosity. He does not rule as a dictator, because many decisions are made by councils within the clans. For more important matters, each tribe has a council of high-ranking Bedouin. If the tribe becomes discontented with the leadership of a sheikh, they may decide to replace him.

After a council meeting, Bedouin men gather for a feast.

Camel raiding and tribal war

In the distant past the Bedouin living in Arabia were convinced that they would obtain reward in heaven if they died when in the service of Allah. They attacked those peoples whom they regarded as "non-believers" in their religion of Islam. Those whom they conquered were given the choice of either converting to Islam or paying taxes. The Bedouin became known as fierce

This is how the Muslim armies were depicted preparing for battle in medieval times.

A Bedouin shepherd does not carry a crook, but a submachine gun. Feuds between tribes still occur.

fighters, and many cities under attack decided that it would be safer to surrender to them.

The religion of Islam was preached by the Prophet Muhammad in Arabia in the seventh century A.D. After his death his followers, known as Muslims, moved into Egypt, Syria, Iraq and other surrounding areas to extend the Muslim world.

For many centuries the Bedouin went on camel-raiding expeditions. They aimed to take camels from the herds of distant tribes, which would find it difficult to retaliate by stealing camels from them. Raiding parties could be small or consist of several hundred men. The Bedouin enjoyed the excitement of these raids, which might extend over 500 miles (800 kilometers) and last for months.

Sometimes one tribe would go to war against another tribe, and on occasions several tribes joined together to fight a common enemy. Such tribal wars were common in Arabia until the end of the nineteenth century. An army might consist of thousands of armed Bedouin. The lance was a traditional weapon used by the camel riders.

Some tribes had hundreds of different coats of mail, and tribesmen fighting on foot carried shields made of hide. By the early twentieth century rifles were widely used in the desert. Often there was great loss of life, a situation that grew more serious as weapons became more sophisticated. By the 1930s, the use of armored cars and airplanes radically altered desert warfare.

13

Honor and hospitality

Bedouin life was governed by strict rules of behavior. One tribe could not suddenly go to war against another tribe without first declaring hostilities, since to attack without any warning would shame the attackers. Even the practice of raiding other tribes to steal camels was governed by codes of honor. It was thought to be fairer to attack a tribe at sunrise, as this would allow them a whole day to track the attackers

A Bedouin woman offers tea to her guests. The Bedouin are renowned for their hospitality.

A town Bedouin (center) visits family members who offer him strong coffee served in Bedouin style.

and try to get the camels back.

Women and children would not be harmed in any attack. A night attack would be regarded as shameful. Bedouin believe that when they sleep, their souls escape through their nostrils. A sleeping person is thought of as almost dead since sleeping people have no souls. Because a person cannot defend himself without a soul, it is forbidden to kill any sleeping person.

A Bedouin will always make a visitor welcome in his tent, and no guest, wanted or unwanted, may be harmed. Hospitality is an important part of life in the desert, and so a stranger may approach any tent and know that he will find rest and refreshment for up to three days. Even an enemy will be allowed to leave the camp in peace.

Guests are given a rug on which to rest and a glass of sweet tea or coffee. The coffee has a greenish color and is flavored with cardamom. There is much ceremony involved in preparing tea or coffee. If the guest is very important, an animal will be killed and cooked in the visitor's honor.

15

Food and drink

Food is seldom plentiful in the desert. Milk and milk products form a major part of the Bedouin diet, along with cereals such as wheat. When grazing is adequate, a camel is able to suckle her young and also

Bread is an important part of the Bedouin diet.

give as much as one gallon (almost four liters) of milk a day for the Bedouin to use.

The main meal is taken in the evening. The men and women eat separately, in different parts of the tent. Everyone sits with one leg beneath him and the other leg with raised knee in front on which to rest his arms. The Bedouin eat only with their right hands.

Main meals may consist of rice that is flavored with clarified butter. Loaves of flat, round bread are baked over the fire on a convex metal baking tray. Canned food, such as fish or tomato paste, is available in many places. Dates are commonly eaten, usually at the end of the meal. Generally, fruits are now more easily available from markets. Locusts can be cooked before being eaten or ground up raw and kept for food flavoring.

The less wealthy Bedouin rarely eat meat. Mutton and the meat of young male camels are enjoyed on special occasions such as feasts prepared to celebrate weddings, or for special visitors.

In the past, water was drawn by hand from a well and poured into bags made of camel skin and carried back to the tent by camel. Nowadays, trucks are often used to transport water from a well. It is then stored in old oil drums.

Bunches of dates are picked from date palm trees and can be eaten fresh, or dried and stored.

Superstition

The Bedouin people were traditionally very superstitious and very religious. They believed that it was necessary to guard against the curse of the Evil Eye.

To avoid this curse they made many charms and amulets, often shaped like hands. Written words from the Qur'an, especially the name of Allah, were powerful charms. The visiting religious teachers, known as *figis*, would write the words down and the Bedouin would wear the pieces of paper in a leather purse around their necks. Camels and tents were decorated with charms to help to keep them from harm. There are some taboo words that Bedouin must not speak for fear or bringing bad luck.

The charms and amulets can still be found today, but the superstitions are gradually having less impact among settled Bedouins.

Left *This Bedouin woman is wearing amulets shaped like hands to ward off evil.*

Below *A group of Bedouin women discussing superstitions.*

Chapter 2 **Surviving in the desert**

Houses made of hair

To make tents, camel or goat hair is collected by combing the animals. It is then woven into long strips which are sewn together. In the Sahara, sheep's wool is used. When wet, it expands to keep rain out. The largest piece is used for the tent roof. The side walls and the back can be rolled up to allow cool breezes to blow through the tent.

The tent is low-lying to prevent winds and sandstorms from blowing it over. Although it is possible to stand up inside, people tend to sit down to avoid smoke from the fire. A wealthy sheikh may have a tent with four or five central poles instead of the two or three used to support

The Bedouin weave cloth from camel or goat hair, or sheep's wool.

Long strips of woven cloth are sewn together to make the tents.

smaller tents. The poles can be raised or lowered depending on the strength of the wind. Smaller poles are used to support the front, the back and the sides.

A curtain inside the tent divides the space into male and female areas. The male section is the more public area with a fireplace around which people can sit and where coffee is made. Camel saddles and cushions are used for seating. The female area is used for storing spare clothes, sacks of grain, dates, coffee beans, and leather bags containing water and cooking utensils. There may also be a paraffin lamp, a radio and perhaps a sewing machine.

Whether tent strips are bought or made, repairs need to be made and the whole tent may have to be taken apart each year so damaged strips can be replaced. There may be only a few tents in a camp or as many as thirty. These family groups move off together every week or two when they need to find fresh grazing areas. The tent and everything inside can be dismantled and packed in less than two hours.

It was once possible to tell how rich a Bedouin was by the number of camels he could afford to keep.

Herders of camels

Camels have been essential for the survival of the Bedouin in the inner desert. One-humped camels are bred in large numbers and have provided many of the necessities of life for the Bedouin. The camel — *jamal* in Arabic — is able to live in very hot conditions. Camels have an unpleasant smell but this does not appear to bother the Bedouin. An animal in good condition has a firm hump in which its fats are stored. The favored color for camels in Syria, Jordan and in the north of Saudi Arabia is white, although in the past sandy-colored camels were

more useful. White camels could not be used in raids as they had no camouflage and could therefore be seen over long distances. In the south of Saudi Arabia, black or dark brown camels are highly prized.

In winter, when there is plenty of grazing, a camel can go for up to six weeks without water. In summer it needs water every three days. Some camel herders travel nearly 2,500 miles (4,000 kilometers) during a typical year.

Female camels, which are stronger and more courageous than males, are used for riding. They can gallop at about 12 miles per hour (20 kph) and if necessary are able to continue at high speed for several hours. Males are used as beasts of burden, carrying heavy loads.

Camels not only provide Bedouin with transportation but also with milk, hair, meat and hide. Their dung is used as fuel for the campfire. The Bedouin use camel urine to wash their hair because it leaves it shiny and kills head lice.

Camels often live for more than twenty years. Many families own herds of up to fifty camels, and wealthier nomads may own many more. Each animal is branded with a *wasm*, which is an owner's identification mark, of which there are thousands of different designs. A camel's forelegs are tied with rope at night to prevent it from straying.

The camel is a stubborn animal. If the load it carries is too heavy, it will sit down and refuse to move.

Sheep and goat herders

The Bedouin who live on the desert fringes often keep sheep and goats alongside or instead of camels. There are many more sheep than camels in the desert. Sheep and goats need grass on which to graze, and they must be kept in places where the rainfall is fairly regular. Sheep, unlike camels, need to drink water every day. This meant that in the past sheep breeding was restricted to the outer desert areas such as the foothills of mountains.

The inner desert areas were used for grazing in spring, after the winter rains. Agricultural stubble was used as food for the herds in autumn. Now shepherds are able to transport water to their flocks by truck. In some places they even take their flocks by truck across barren desert in order to find suitable grazing.

In the past, flocks of only sixty sheep were quite common, but larger flocks are now being built up in many areas.

A goat herd rests in the welcome shade of a tree.

Above *A fox scavenges for food in the harsh desert.*

Above *Falconry is a popular pastime with the Bedouin.*

Above *Bedouin children play with the family saluki dog.*

Hunting

Many parts of the desert were once filled with herds of gazelle, oryx, hyena, ostriches, wolves and foxes. There are now few wild animals to be seen and even rabbits, hares and jerboas are rare. They have all been hunted indiscriminately by towns people in large hunting parties equipped with cars, rifles and even submachine guns.

Some animals are now extinct in the wild, although breeding stocks of such creatures as the oryx are being built up in conservation zones. Hunting in the Arabian desert is now illegal.

The Bedouin, who once hunted animals for food, now find that sporting expeditions from the towns have reduced the chances of finding wild animals. For many years the Bedouin have hunted on camel, with saluki dogs to help them find prey. The dogs travel on the camel with the rider until prey is sighted. The Bedouins are also expert at training falcons. They use them to hunt fox, hare, partridge and quail.

This woman is gathering food for the camels from a cultivated patch of land.

Cultivating the land

Sheep-herding Bedouin need to move about much less frequently than camel herders, since they are able to stay for longer periods on one site with their flocks. For part of the year they may live in houses in a village, keeping chickens and growing grain crops for their own use and alfalfa for their sheep.

The Bedouin grow crops in the deserts of Negev, Sinai and the Sahara. The specific location may change from year to year, depending on which areas have had rainfall. Farming techniques are simple. Seed is scattered on the damp earth and then plowed into the ground, with perhaps a camel pulling the plow. If there is a good harvest, the surplus grain is stored in pits lined with straw and covered with wet clay. This soon dries hard and protects the grain until it is needed.

A *wadi* is a valley where rainfall runs off the hills in the desert and soaks into the ground. The surrounding area can be cultivated by farmers who sink wells until they reach this water. These oases are able to support enough vegetation to grow such crops as grain, tobacco and vegetables. These crops are often grown under date palms, which provide shade from the strong sun.

26

The Bedouin harvest crops of dates in late summer.

Bedouin

Many Bedouin camp close to an oasis in the late summer, which is when the dates are harvested. Dates are very important in the desert since they nourish the Bedouin as well as their dogs and horses. The Bedouin dry dates and store them or eat them fresh from the trees.

27

The blue tattoo marks and silver braclets are traditional.

Clothing

It may seem strange that the Bedouin, living in such hot, dry conditions, cover themselves completely with clothing. They do this because their skin would suffer if exposed to the sun, so clothing is worn as protection against its rays as well as against blowing sand. Bedouin garments are loose and comfortable. Air circulates easily under them, reducing the amount of sweating and providing a cool layer near the body. Only their hands, feet and part of their faces are exposed to the sun.

Males wear a cotton garment like a long shirt. This may be white, brown or gray. A small cap is worn on the head, over which is placed a *Keffiyeh*, a cloth of white, red and white, or black and white. This is kept in position with a double band of black cord. It helps to protect the neck and head from the sand and sun. In chilly weather, or for important meetings, they wear a long, woolen cloak that might be sleeveless and is usually black, brown or cream. On very cold days a sheepskin coat may be worn.

Females wear long dresses, sometimes two at a time, reaching to their ankles, with long sleeves to protect their arms. The traditional dresses are a dark blue color. Hand-embroidered dresses are sometimes made by the Bedouin in Syria, but in most Arab countries garments are now made from brightly colored

This man runs a market stall selling only Keffiyeh, *the traditional Arab headdress.*

man-made materials. Some Bedouin women cover their faces with a veil made of black material with eye slots from which they can peer out. In the past it was the custom for all women living in towns to be veiled in this way when they left their homes. Although many Bedouin still wear these veils, in the north of Saudi Arabia most women do not cover their faces. Jewelry as well as eye makeup is often worn, and many women have blue tattoo marks on their faces and use henna to paint patterns on their hands.

Both men and women wear their hair very long. It was once the custom for men to braid hair at the sides of their faces.

Chapter 3 **Changes in Bedouin lifestyles**

Bedouin women in Iraq fill cans with water brought to them by a government tanker once every two weeks.

The changing desert

At one time, Bedouin guides were needed to conduct travelers safely across the desert. The Bedouin were skilled in finding the way as well as in tracking animals and men. They could judge the age of the tracks, and perhaps even identify a particular person from them. Now roads of good quality have been built in many places and there are maps to guide

motorists. The deserts can now be crossed by motor vehicles, and airplanes have made remote places accessible.

Trucks are often used in herding. Water can be transported in barrels or large cans to flocks and herds. The animals themselves can be moved to better grazing by transporting them in larger vehicles. A camel can be moved from one place to another in the back of a small pick-up truck. On some migrations, trucks are even loaded with all a family's belongings including the tent, the firewood, water containers and the family itself.

As a result of government projects large, deep wells have been sunk using advanced drilling methods. These wells may be used by all Bedouin. This has ended arguments about water rights, and small communities have grown up beside these wells. But the Bedouin who choose to stay in camps within traveling distance of the new wells sometimes overgraze the land and this causes problems.

In the past, each tribe often had its own distinct territory — or *dirah* — in the desert, over which it had rights of pasture and of water from wells. The newer method of land use, which is known as *hema*, allows unrestricted grazing in any area. Nomads do not now bother about conserving pasture if they feel that the next group to come along will overgraze the land.

Water is still drawn by hand from some wells.

Trucks can travel faster than camels and carry heavier loads.

The impact of oil

The Arab countries were fairly poor before the discovery of oil. Now instead of simply being places where animal herders live, the Arab countries have suddenly had to adjust to becoming some of the richest lands in the world. The international companies arrived and quickly began to construct oil wells. In this new world of high technology and rapid change, the camel is not as important as it was in the past. A car can travel faster than a camel, and a truck can carry far heavier loads.

Oil production became very important in various countries of the Arabian peninsula in the 1950s and 1960s. Profits made from the

exploitation of oil have allowed the governments to spend vast amounts of money to find new supplies of water, as well as improve housing, education and public health.

The countries of the Middle East are members of OPEC — the Organization of Petroleum Exporting Countries. Oil has given great prosperity to these lands. Scientists are now trying to find other minerals, and governments are encouraging the growth of new industries in order to provide alternative sources of income and employment when all the oil is gone.

The extraction of oil has brought far-reaching changes to many people living in the Middle East. But most of the wealth has gone to the people

A Bedouin from the desert visits Abud Dhabi — a city built on sand.

living in towns. Some Bedouin have benefited, but they tend to spend any money that comes their way rather than save or invest it. This means that there is now a considerable difference between the living standard of nomadic Bedouin and that of town-dwellers. Many of the nomads are unable to read and write, and know little about the world other than caring for camels, goats and sheep in the desert.

A variety of occupations

Today not all Bedouin tend sheep, goats or camels or cultivate crops. When oil companies began to employ local Bedouin to help work their oil wells, some tribesmen preferred to receive regular wages rather than herd animals. Some Bedouin families decided to stay in one place instead of moving around. When pasture became scarce, they

Many Bedouin join the Jordan Arab Legion. Their knowledge of the desert can be very useful.

The Saudi-Bahrain oil pipeline has brought work to many Bedouin.

sold their animals. Many Bedouin settled permanently in the main oil-producing areas. Others found jobs in cities, and many work for their governments. Some have become truck or taxi drivers, or have entered the police force and the army.

The Jordan Arab Legion enlists many Bedouin. These soldiers use not only camels and horses but also jeeps. They must accept that loyalty to their king and country is more important than to the tribal sheikh. In Saudi Arabia the National Guard, which is responsible for internal security, is made up mostly of Bedouin soldiers. The Bedouin knowledge of the desert is often very useful in these jobs.

In some areas virtually every male Bedouin has held a job and earned wages, even if only on a temporary basis. Bedouin who live near the borders of other countries may do some smuggling of livestock between one country and another because the borders cannot be checked continually at all points.

The Bedouin have always needed some money to buy some of the basic necessities of life. However, in the cash society of today they need money even more than they did in the past. Motor vehicles and gasoline must be paid for with hard cash, so must such luxuries as cooking stoves and battery-operated television sets for use in their tents.

Standards of living

The nomadic Bedouin who visit the town markets, known as *souks*, find an increasing variety of supplies and luxuries offered for sale. Many of them have cash they obtain from the sale of some of their animals. The standard of living of many Bedouin has improved greatly over the years. Wage earners have the security of a regular income, and even those who still herd animals do not have the worry of suddenly losing their herds now that raiding parties are illegal.

In Saudi Arabia about half the population used to be nomadic. That country still has the largest proportion of Bedouin in any Arab country, although significant numbers leave the desert each year and settle in permanent homes.

The physical well-being of many Bedouin has improved following the building of many clinics and hospitals. Camps are visited by

Bedouin women shop in a souk — *an Arab marketplace.*

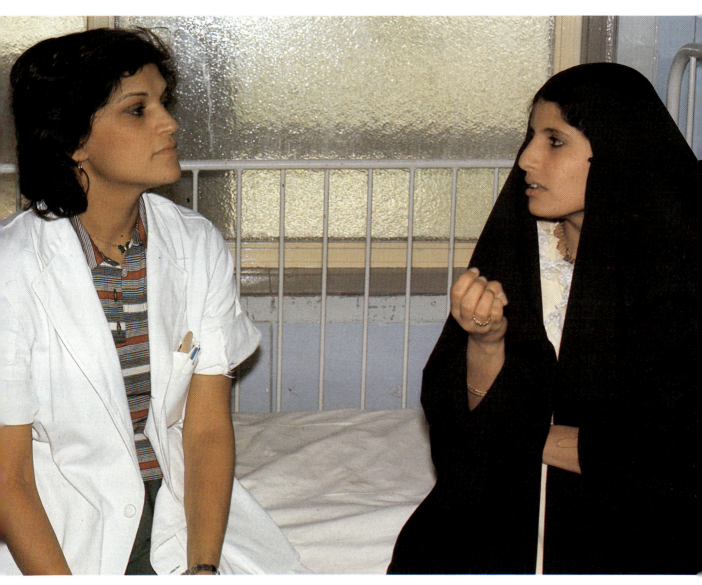

Hospitals in several countries try to encourage the Bedouin to use their medical services. Here a doctor listens to a patient's problems.

doctors and nurses who teach the Bedouin the importance of vaccination and medicine. Despite this, many tribesmen still believe in the traditional magic charms and spells, including burning diseased areas of the body.

In order to encourage the Bedouin to use medical services correctly, one hospital in Oman has built wards especially for nomads. These wards give the impression of outdoor life, and the family of the sick person is allowed to camp nearby. This hospital has been very successful in helping the Bedouin.

Chapter 4

The Bedouin today

Settlement and integration

In recent years governments have actively encouraged nomads to settle. King Abdul Aziz Ibn Saud, who founded Saudi Arabia in the early twentieth century, claimed to be "King of the Bedouin." He provided the Bedouin with land to cultivate in the hope that this would tie them down to living a settled life.

The plan did not always succeed, since the work was hard and water supplies were inadequate for farming. Many Bedouin who tried the settled life felt lost and unhappy at first. The shanty town areas where they tended to take up residence quickly became unsanitary.

Some people believe that the Bedouin will settle more easily if the change is a slow one — perhaps from camel to sheep herding, and from there to a semi-settled life in a camp before becoming permanent members of a village. Others think that the change should be made quickly and in one sharp move from desert to town.

Most nomadic families have at least a few relatives who have abandoned the desert and now live in towns. Many of them have become "invisible" Bedouin, dressing in much the same clothes as other town-dwellers. In the outer desert areas more Bedouin now drive trucks than ride camels.

The governments have provided the Bedouin tribes with financial subsidies in order to improve their standard of living and to show that they understand the problems nomads have to face. The paramount sheikh of a tribe often lives in a house in a city and works as a mediator between the tribesmen and the government.

King Abdul Aziz Ibn Saud claimed to be "King of the Bedouin."

The governments show some responsibility for the nomads, but at the same time, dislike having numbers of Bedouin wandering around the country at will. It is difficult to collect taxes from them, and often they need to be considered separately from other citizens of the country. For example, at election time it may be necessary to send mobile polling stations into the desert to collect votes from the Bedouin a few days before the official voting day. This is done in order to contact as many of them as possible.

Some Bedouin today live a semi-settled life in shanty towns.

Education

Increasing numbers of Bedouin settle each year in low, concrete houses in villages and towns, and in apartment blocks in cities. They need to learn how to use electric appliances, water faucets, and even how to flush toilets. There may be a period of uncertainty before they become properly integrated into the local community. It is not unknown for new homeowners to pitch tents next to the house, using the house for their animals and the tent for themselves. Concrete floors seem cold and uninviting compared with carpets placed on sand. Even such apparently simple furniture as tables, chairs and beds makes their lifestyle radically different from life in a tent.

It is becoming common to see women sitting in the same room as men, with a television in the corner and paintings hanging on the wall. These are all indications of rapid changes and show that the Bedouin are moving quickly from an ancient to a modern lifestyle.

As part of a re-education plan, houses have been built to encourage Bedouin to settle in one place.

Children work at the blackboard in a school in the Sinai Desert, Egypt.

Educating the Bedouin to live in towns is an important process. Free schooling has been greatly extended in recent decades. Saudi Arabia, for example, began a Five Year Plan in 1975 aimed at doubling the number of pupils by 1980. This allowed all boys and half the girls to attend elementary schools, and further progress has been made since.

Young children often go to village schools. Older pupils may have the chance to go to an urban secondary school or a night school. The nomads living in remote areas send their children to stay with relatives living near a school, or to a school for Bedouin pupils. Some teachers visit the tribes and even travel with them, but many children living in isolated areas still do not get a proper or extended education.

41

This Bedouin family moved from a tent to this modern house, but they still keep camels.

Changing attitudes

The Bedouin have always believed in the superiority of their nomadic lifestyle over all others. Such ideas, however, have had to be reassessed over recent years, and attitudes are now altering radically among the Bedouin. These changes can be seen in many aspects of their daily life. For example, men often wear trousers bought at the local market, but they still wear the traditional headgear.

Even nomadic Bedouin are gradually collecting more possessions, and as these accumulate it becomes more difficult to move from place to place. As a result, families often prefer to change campsites as seldom as possible.

Another change is that camels are disappearing now that alternative forms of transportation are available for both riders and possessions. Consequently, many former camel herders keep sheep since they are more profitable and easier to tend. The nomads today are not always families. Many are employees who are paid to look after herds and flocks belonging to other people.

In Syria, these two Bedouin women are paid to milk and tend a flock of sheep that belongs to someone else.

Chapter 5 The future of the Bedouin

Bedouin in a Jordan street wear Western-style trousers with the traditional Arab Keffiyeh.

It is sometimes said that in a few years there will be no more Bedouin living in tents in the desert. It seems likely, however, that some will continue to live in the old ways. The production of meat and milk are still important occupations, and there are few other uses for such poor land. Young people are continuing to leave the desert, and this means that those left behind are often the elderly who find difficulty in coping with the jobs that need to be done.

Perhaps the more important,

larger tribes are those most likely to survive in a new age. It is the poor Bedouin and the wealthy who might be most likely to move from the desert to the towns, leaving their tents for the comforts associated with progress.

It is possible that the number of Bedouin in the Middle East is now only about one percent of the total population living in these countries. In Saudi Arabia about eight out of ten people now live in towns and cities such as Riyadh, Jeddah, Mecca, Taif and Medina.

Perhaps the rest of the world has something to learn from Bedouin attitudes. They seldom rush since the heat slows them down and they believe that hurrying is the work of the devil. They do not worry too much about what they cannot alter, for they believe that tomorrow is in the hands of Allah.

This Bedouin enjoys the stillness of the desert.

Glossary

Alfalfa A plant used to feed animals.

Allah The Muslim name of God.

Amulet Something worn as a charm to guard against evil.

Cardamom A spice made from seeds, used for flavoring food.

Clarified butter Butter that is heated and skimmed and then keeps for long periods.

Council A group of people in authority who meet to make decisions.

Desert A dry, barren region.

Exploitation Making full use of a natural resource without worrying about the consequences.

Henna A red dye used as decoration.

Hyena A meat-eating animal related to the dog family.

Illicit Unlawful.

Jerboas Small desert rodents with long hind legs.

Lance A long wooden weapon with a sharp metal tip at one end.

Locusts Winged insects.

Migration Moving from one place to another.

Nomads People who wander in search of pasture for their animals.

Oasis (plural Oases) A place in the desert where there is enough water for vegetation and where crops may be grown by irrigating the land.

Oryx A large antelope with straight horns.

Paramount The most important.

Quail A bird, similar to a partridge, that is hunted for food.

Saluki A breed of dog resembling a greyhound.

Shanty town An area of simple, crudely built houses.

Subsidy A grant of money.

Taboo Something that is forbidden for religious or social reasons.

Territory An area of land under the control of a tribe or ruler.

Glossary of Arabic words

Arab Sheep and goat herders.

Badawiyin Camel herders.

Bani People who belong to one tribe.

Dirah An area of land over which certain people had the right to graze animals and draw water.

Figis Wandering religious teachers who would visit the Bedouin in the desert.

Hadari Settled tribesmen.

Hema A system that opens grazing land to anyone who wants to use it.

Jamal A camel. There are also many other more specialized words.

Keffiyeh A cloth worn on the head to protect against the sun.

Kohl A dark-colored powder used as eye makeup.

Sheikh The elected chief of an Arab tribe.

Souk The marketplace in an Arab town.

Wadi A valley that has underground water from rainfall running from the hills.

Wasm An identification mark to show ownership of a camel.

Books to read

Veiled Sentiments: Honor and Poetry in a Bedouin Society by Lila Abu-Lughod (University of California Press, 1987).

The Herders of Cyrenaica: Ecology, Economy, and Kinship Among the Bedouin of Eastern Libya by Roy Behnke (University of Illinois Press, 1980).

Bedouin Tribes of the Euphrates by Anne Blunt (Biblio Distributors, 1968).

The Camel and the Wheel by Richard Bulliet (Harvard University Press, 1975).

From Camel to Truck: the Bedouin in the Modern World by Dawn Chatty (Vantage, 1985).

The Arab of the Desert by H.R. Dickson (Allen Unwin, 1983).

A Bedouin Boyhood by Isaak Diqs Universe, 1969).

Bedouin by Wayne Eastep (University of Pennsylvania Press, 1985).

Living Among the Bedouin Arabs by Alex R. Johnson (Vantage, 1985).

The Bedouin by Shirley Kay (David and Charles, 1978).

Sons of Ishmael: A Study of the Egyptian Bedouin by George W. Murray (AMS Press, 1935).

Bedouins by Stella Peters (Silver).

Black Tents of Arabia by Carl R. Raswan (Folcroft, 1947).

A Closer Look at the Bedouin by Fidelity Lancaster (Hamish Hamilton, 1978).

The Seven Pillars of Wisdom by T.E. Lawrence (Jonathan Cape, 1935).

Arabian Sands by Wilfred Thesiger (Longman, 1959).

Picture Acknowledgments

The photographs in this book were supplied by the following: Christine Osborne 8, 9, 10, 13, 15, 18, 19, 22, lower left 25, right 25, 29, 30, 32, 33, 34, 35, 36, 37, 40, 42, 43, 44. Laura Zito *front cover and frontispiece*, 7, 11, 14, 16, 17, 20, 21, 23, 24, upper left 25, 26, 27, 28, 31, 39, 41, 45. Ministry of Information, Kingdom of Saudi Arabia, 38. Map on page 6 by Malcolm Walker. Illustration on page 12 from a medieval illustrated manuscript, Wayland Picture Library.

Index